# FAMILIES

© Aladdin Books 1992

*First published in the United States
in 1992 by*
Gloucester Press
95 Madison Avenue
New York, NY 10016

Library of Congress
Cataloging-in-Publication Data

Ganeri, Anita, 1961-
Families / by Anita Ganeri.
p.     cm. — (Animal behavior)
Includes index.
Summary: Examines how different
kinds of animals reproduce and
raise their young.
ISBN 0-531-17364-X
1. Familial behavior in
animals—Juvenile literature.
2. Animal behavior—Juvenile
literature. [1. Familial behavior in
animals. 2. Parental behavior in
animals. 3. Animals—Habits and
behavior.] I. Title. II. Series:
Animal behavior (New York, N.Y.)
QL761.5.G36     1992b
591.56—dc20
92-6798     CIP     AC

The author, Anita Ganeri, has
written many books for children
on natural history and other topics.

The consultant, Steve Parker, has
a degree in zoology and has written
more than 50 books for children on
science and nature.

**Design:** David West
Children's Book Design
**Designer:** John Kelly
**Editor:** Jen Green
**Picture researcher:** Emma Krikler
**Illustrator:** Joanne Cowne

**Photocredits**
All the pictures in this book
have been supplied by Bruce
Coleman Limited apart from
the following: Cover
and page 29: Planet Earth
Pictures; page 6: Mary Evans
Picture Library; pages 9 and
25 bottom: Natural History
Picture Agency; page 22

# ANIMAL BEHAVIOR

# FAMILIES

ANITA GANERI

**GLOUCESTER PRESS**
New York · London · Toronto · Sydney

# CONTENTS

# INTRODUCTION

A family is a group consisting of parents and offspring. It may also involve other relatives, such as uncles, aunts, cousins, nephews, and nieces. Many animals live in families, whether in a large group, such as a flock, swarm, or herd, or in a small, closely-knit unit.

## Family ties

The main purpose of all animal families is to produce offspring and make sure that the young have the best possible chance of survival. But different species of animals have very different family structures. Chimpanzees live in close-knit families, 15-20 strong. These groups contain male and female chimps and young of various ages. The family cooperates in finding food and a place to sleep and in defending the young and the family's patch of forest, or territory. The bond between young chimps and their mothers is strong, often lasting until the young are up to 15 years old.

Wild horses live in much looser-knit groups. The horses are not closely related to each other. They tend to leave the group of their birth and spend their lives in another group.

## Leaving well alone

Many kinds of animals do not belong to a family group. For example, no parental care is provided for the millions of eggs laid at a time by the female cod. The eggs are fertilized by the male cod, and then abandoned to float near the surface of the sea until they hatch. Nearly all the eggs are eaten by predators before they reach adulthood.

Chimpanzee mothers spend a great deal of time and energy looking after their offspring.

# WHY HAVE FAMILIIES?

**The main aim of an animal's habits and behavior is to breed and produce offspring, who will grow up to continue the species. By protecting and feeding their young in a family group, parents increase their offspring's chances of survival so that they, in turn, can one day reproduce.**

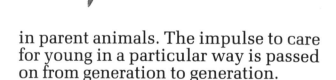

When animals mate, they pass on characteristics, such as the length of their limbs and the shape of their teeth, to their young. These characteristics are conveyed by genes, the tiny particles in cells which carry the instructions on how the body grows and functions, and which pass from parent to offspring.

If an animal possesses a quality that enables it to hunt or to avoid predators particularly well, it is more likely to survive, breed, and pass on this quality to its own offspring. Over many generations, a gene that provides a good survival feature becomes more widespread in the species. This process of gradual change in living things is called evolution by natural selection.

Natural selection applies to physical features such as horns and teeth. It also affects behavior, such as caring qualities in parent animals. The impulse to care for young in a particular way is passed on from generation to generation.

**Who cares?**

Many animals, such as the millions of worms, snails, and starfish, receive no care from their parents. Other animals are reared in family groups. The degree of care varies from species to species. Some animals clean, feed, carry, and defend their young until they are old enough to fend for themselves, and even after this.

The number of offspring an animal has determines the kind of care it can provide for its young. Animals that produce thousands of young at one time cannot offer the individual care that can be given to a few babies. Many fish and insects put all their energy into mass production. They produce thousands of eggs, so that some, at least, will survive. Parents who invest large amounts of energy in caring for their young have fewer babies, but give each a much better chance of survival.

The idea of natural selection was first suggested by the English naturalist Charles Darwin in 1859.

About half of male scrub jays never breed themselves. But they help to feed the chicks in their family, and protect them from predators such as snakes.

A male ostrich mates with several females. He incubates all the eggs in one nest, guarding up to 40 eggs and keeping them warm! When the chicks hatch, they follow their father wherever he goes. If two males meet and squabble, one may run away. His chicks then follow the other male.

### Family help

Scrub jays of Florida live in families of up to a dozen adult birds. Family members all work to raise new chicks. The parents are assisted by up to six helpers, usually males from a previous clutch of eggs. They help to find food for their younger sisters and brothers, and defend them from predators.

Some young animals are looked after by both parents; others are cared for by their mother or father alone. The kind of behavior that has evolved in each particular species offers the best chance of survival for that species.

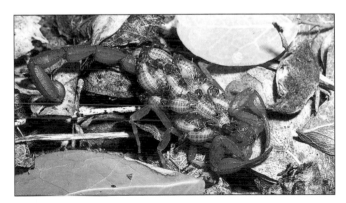

If young scorpions fall off their mother's back, she will wait for them to climb back on again.

### Single parents

Young desert scorpions are looked after by their mother. After mating, she lays her eggs which hatch almost at once. Then the young scorpions climb up their mother's pincers onto her back. They cling on tightly with their tiny legs and pincers and are carried and protected in this way until they are old enough to fend for themselves.

Ostrich chicks trot obediently after their father, who keeps a lookout for food and danger.

# INSTINCT AND LEARNING

**Animal parents and young behave largely according to instinct – knowledge which is in-built from birth and does not need to be learned. Young animals also learn by watching and copying their parents and other family members and by playing among themselves.**

These ducklings have imprinted on their mother, and follow her in single file.

A female tree shrew gives birth to between one and three young. She marks them with a special smell which identifies them as her babies. This smell makes the difference between the babies surviving or being eaten by their parent. If they are not marked, the mother shrew will identify them only as a nourishing meal and eat them.

**Like domestic kittens, cheetah and lion cubs learn to hunt through play. They use their mother and each other as targets, and will also chase after small moving objects that catch their eye.**

## Recognizing mother
When a gosling hatches, it follows the first moving thing it sees, which is usually its mother. The gosling follows wherever she goes and copies her actions. This process is called imprinting. In experiments with greylag goslings, the Austrian naturalist Konrad Lorenz discovered that imprinting is instinctive. If the first thing a gosling sees is a human being, for example, it will follow it as mother instead. Lorenz's theory was proved when a clutch of goslings imprinted on him!

## How not to be eaten
Parents must also be able to recognize their young. Ants live in large colonies, and identify their relatives in the nest by smell. Each colony seems to have a distinctive smell derived from its food.

## Playing and learning
A wolf cub knows instinctively that it should hunt, but it learns how to do so by copying its parents and through play. In mock fights with its brothers and sisters, it develops movements and techniques which will help it in adult life. Cheetah and lion cubs practice their hunting techniques by pouncing on the end of their mother's tail.

Some animal parents help their offspring to develop skills by bringing them half-dead prey to practice on. Young otters play with fish which their mother has brought to the pool. Their game involves practicing the diving and swimming skills which they will need as adult underwater hunters.

**Play reinforces the bonds among otter young and between the parents and their offspring.**

### "Learning" to fly

Birds are born with a great deal of in-built knowledge. They know how to build their nests and raise their young instinctively. They also know how to fly instinctively, when the time is right. However, fledglings of some species, such as eagles, spend time on the edges of their nests, flapping outstretched wings to practice their flight movements. Eagles rely heavily on their flying skills for hunting and in courtship rituals, so perhaps it is important to get these movements perfect!

# MOTHER IN CHARGE

**Young animals of many species are looked after by their mothers, who raise their offspring on their own. This is the most common form of parental care among birds and mammals.**

Female animals usually put far more energy and resources into producing young and caring for them than males do. In mammals (animals that suckle their offspring with milk) this is because the female is physically adapted to feed the young, and the male is not. The care offered by some animal mothers gives their offspring a high chance of survival. For the mothers it means that their genes are likely to survive and be passed on to the next generation.

### Growing up on the ice

Polar bear cubs are born in an ice cave under the Arctic snow in the middle of winter. They spend the first few months of their lives there, in a den dug by their mother. The cubs are born blind, helpless, and tiny. They suckle on their mother's rich milk until they are old enough to leave the den and follow her on hunting trips across the ice. The cubs stay with the mother until they are about two and a half years old.

### Carried away

After mating, the female wolf spider spins a silk sac around her eggs. The sac remains attached to her spinnerets (the silk-producing glands on her abdomen). When she goes out hunting, she drags the sac about with her until the young spiders hatch. Then she carries the babies on her back until they can look after themselves.

**The female wolf spider takes her eggs with her, rather than leaving them unprotected.**

**Alligators and crocodiles are unusual among reptiles in the amount of care they give their young. Mothers guard their nests and eggs from predators, and keep a close watch over the hatchlings.**

**Polar bear cubs are well grown by the time they leave their den, but stay close to their mother.**

Female alligators and crocodiles were once thought to eat their young, because they were observed with their babies in their jaws. In fact, crocodile and alligator mothers carry their newly hatched young in their mouths from the nest site on the river or lake bank, to a stretch of water which will act as the "nursery." The females continue to look after their offspring until the young are a few months old.

**Mother earwigs sit over their eggs like birds. They may have up to 50 eggs in one clutch.**

## On guard
Most insects abandon their eggs as soon as they have laid them, but the female earwig is an unusually caring mother. She lays her eggs in a burrow in the ground, and guards them until they hatch. She turns and cleans the eggs to keep them free from parasites. For a few days after they hatch, she continues to protect the young from attack, sheltering them under her body if necessary.

## Parents in paradise
Compared to the male in his brightly colored breeding plumage, the female bird of paradise is very drab indeed. But the plumage of both sexes serves a particular purpose. The male shows off his bright feathers in the hope of attracting a mate. The gaudier he is, the greater are his chances of finding a partner. The female, on the other hand, must build the nest, lay the eggs, and raise the chicks. Her drab colors help to camouflage her from potential predators so that attention is not drawn to her young in the nest.

# THE LONE FATHER

Some young animals are taken care of and reared solely by their father, although this phenomenon is quite rare. This method of care leaves the female free to mate again, or to feed and replace the energy she has used up in producing her offspring.

The male midwife toad carries his load of sticky eggs on his back until they are ready to hatch.

## Minding the eggs

Midwife toad eggs are laid by the female toad, but looked after by the male until they hatch. The female lays her eggs in strings, which the male winds around his back legs. He carries them until they are ready to hatch, a period of up to seven weeks. Then he makes his way to a pond or stream and lowers his back into the water. He remains in this position until the tadpoles hatch out, which can take up to an hour.

Male seahorses incubate their eggs in a pouch on their bellies, which develops several days before mating. As they mate, the female squirts thousands of eggs into the male's pouch, where they are fertilized by his sperm. The eggs remain in the safety of the pouch for about a month. Then they hatch, and the male appears to give birth to hundreds of tiny young seahorses.

Many male birds are more concerned with attracting mates than with looking after eggs. But the female spotted sandpiper leaves the male to incubate the eggs in the nest while she goes off in search of another mate. The male continues to take care of his chicks after they have hatched, leading them on food-finding expeditions.

## Foster fathers

Most animals do not tend to make good foster parents. They are usually reluctant to invest precious energy and time in the care of offspring that are not their own. There are some exceptions to this, however.

Unless the anemone fish fosters his predecessor's eggs, the female refuses to mate with him.

In Japanese anemone fish, it is the male who looks after the eggs until they hatch. If he is driven off or killed by another male, the newcomer takes over his parental duties and raises the eggs as if they were his own. He has an ulterior motive, however! If the newcomer proves himself to be a caring foster father, the mother of the eggs is more likely to mate with him so that he can raise his own eggs.

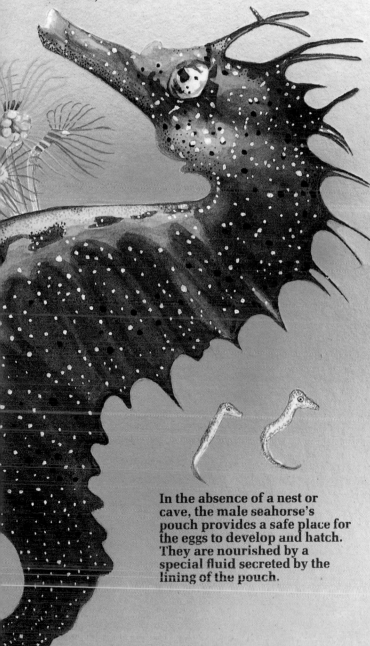

In the absence of a nest or cave, the male seahorse's pouch provides a safe place for the eggs to develop and hatch. They are nourished by a special fluid secreted by the lining of the pouch.

Male lions are caring fathers to their own offspring, but aggressive toward other cubs.

A family group, or pride, of lions is largely made up of female relations and their young. Male lions may stay with the pride, but are kept at a distance. Toward their own cubs, the males are tolerant fathers, even when the cubs are playful. If one male challenges another and wins, however, he will kill the defeated lion's cubs and mate with the females to father his own instead.

13

# TWO-PARENT FAMILIES

**In many animal groups, both parents share the care and protection of their young. The parents may pair for life, or form a partnership for breeding and then separate again. Two-parent care is most common in kinds of animals which are monogamous – where the partners mate only with each other.**

In many species of birds and mammals, care of the young is too much work for one parent on its own. Many birds, for example chaffinches, share these duties. The male and female build the nest together and share the incubation of the eggs. Both birds hunt for food to give their ever-hungry chicks. They search in the woods for caterpillars and other small creatures, which they bring back to the nest. Working together is the only way of making sure that the parents can collect enough food for the chicks and for themselves.

Swans are extremely protective parents. Most swans pair for life. They build their waterside nest together and care for the young. Both parents guide the cygnets on their first winter migration, showing them the route to take and the long-established places to rest on the way.

A flock of swans consists of separate family units of parent birds and their offspring.

The survival of both chaffinch young and parents depends on cooperation between the adult birds.

## Left holding the baby

Marmosets are tiny monkeys which live in the rainforests of South America. The female usually gives birth to twins, which the parents carry on their backs as they search for food among the trees. The female uses up a lot of energy feeding her young on milk and sometimes has little strength left to carry them as well. Then the male takes over, helped by offspring from previous years and by other, unrelated, marmosets.

The king and queen termites'
responsibility is to breed. Most
of the eggs hatch into workers.
The workers' job is to keep the
colony running smoothly, and
they do not breed.

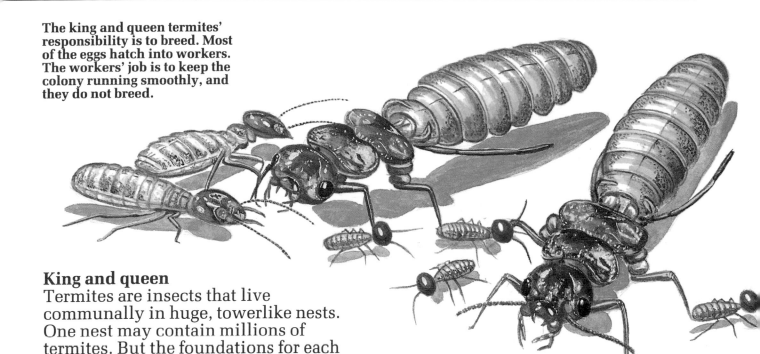

## King and queen

Termites are insects that live
communally in huge, towerlike nests.
One nest may contain millions of
termites. But the foundations for each
colony are laid by one pair of termites —
the king and queen. At certain times of
the year, males and females develop
wings and fly away from their old nests.
If they survive the flight, they pair up,
crawl underground and mate in the
"royal chamber." The first batch of
young are looked after by their parents.
Thereafter, the young look after each
other, and their parents. The royal
couple are the only members of the
colony that can breed. They may
continue to do so for up to 20 years.

## Raising an imposter

Some animals pass the responsibility of
caring for their young onto parents of a
different species. The European cuckoo
lays her eggs in the nests of other birds,
such as warblers or dunnocks. She
removes one of their eggs and replaces it
with her own, which matches the color
of the host bird's eggs. The young
cuckoo is hatched and raised by its
foster parents.

This cuckoo chick has a white
wagtail as its foster parent. It is
already much bigger than the
wagtail. Having pushed the wagtail
chicks out of the nest, it consumes
all the food its
foster parent
brings to the
nest.

# EXTENDED FAMILIES

**In some families, young animals are looked after not only by their parents, but by aunts, uncles, cousins, and older brothers and sisters. In this type of "extended" family, members of the group might well raise young that are not their own offspring.**

A young elephant is protected and cared for by a group of close relations, including aunts and cousins.

## Helping others

The practice of animals helping each other at some cost to themselves is called altruism. At first it seems to contradict Darwin's theory of natural selection, with its suggestion of "every animal for itself," since many animals who help others in their family do not breed themselves and so give up the chance of passing on their genes. In 1964, the naturalist W.D. Hamilton offered the theory of kin selection as an explanation. He suggested that in aiding close relatives, or kin, animals are actually increasing the chances of common, "family" genes surviving.

African elephants live in herds of closely related females. The bonds between these mothers, daughters, and sisters are strong. When a calf is born, all the females become "midwives," helping the baby to its feet and stroking it with their trunks. If its mother dies, one of the baby's "aunts" will adopt it.

Tamarin monkeys from South America live in extended family groups of up to 15 animals. One female breeds each season, then all the members of the family help to carry and feed her young. This gives the young adult "helpers" experience in caring for the young, which will be useful when their own offspring are born.

## Parent sharing

African hunting dogs live in large packs, which can contain over 30 members. The dogs share the tasks of caring for and feeding the pack's young. The pups are raised together, and a mother will suckle any who are hungry, even if they are not her own. When the pups are older, they are fed with meat regurgitated by adults returning from a hunt. This practice continues until the pups are about 14 months old and can fend for themselves.

Adult dholes help care for mothers and pups by bringing them regurgitated meat.

## Keeping order

Macaque monkeys, like many monkeys and apes, bring up their young in extended families. Macaques spend a great deal of time grooming each other's fur, picking off lice, ticks, and dirt. Grooming keeps the monkeys' fur clean and builds harmony within the extended family. Mothers groom their offspring, developing the bonds between them. Grooming also strengthens links within the wider group, helping to establish which animals are in charge without the need for fighting to take place. Grooming reinforces rank within the group, for senior animals are groomed first.

All members of the tamarin family help to look after and carry the young monkeys until they reach adult size at about two years old.

An adult long-tailed macaque grooms an adolescent monkey within its extended family group.

# SAFETY IN NUMBERS

**Huge groups of animals, though not families in the strictest sense, have an important practical value in nature. By living among a large number of its own kind, an animal is often much safer than if it lived on its own.**

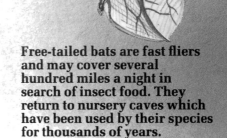

A shoal of fish is a baffling sight. It is difficult for a predator to target an individual.

Free-tailed bats are fast fliers and may cover several hundred miles a night in search of insect food. They return to nursery caves which have been used by their species for thousands of years.

Predators may be confused by the mass of moving stripes as zebras run across the savanna.

## Shoals and herds

Many small fish, such as herring or mackerel, live in vast shoals as a defense against predators, such as tuna or barracuda. A herring shoal may contain millions of fish, all of them almost identical in appearance. This, and the way the shoal moves and changes shape, confuses the predator and makes it very difficult to pick out and catch an individual fish. As a means of defense, being part of a shoal is particularly beneficial in the open sea, where there is nowhere else to hide.

On the open plains of Africa, a solitary zebra would make an easy target for a lion or cheetah. Being part of a large herd is much safer. As the herd grazes, one or other of its members is watching out for enemies at all times and is ready to sound a warning if necessary. It would be more difficult for a lone zebra to feed and keep watch at the same time.

Female free-tailed bats raise their babies inside cave nurseries. The caves become very crowded, with the young bats packed together to keep warm. Bracken Cave in Texas, in the United States, alone contains over 20 million bats! When the mothers return from their nightly search for food, they are somehow able to find and feed their own baby out of the 10 million youngsters available. Inside the cave, the young bats are safe from predators, such as raccoons and bat hawks. Once they leave, however, their lives are in great danger. Over two-thirds of them will be dead before a year has passed.

This kittiwake colony is nesting on a ruined castle wall – a good substitute for a sea cliff.

## Protecting the young

Many seabirds, such as black-headed gulls, nest in huge breeding colonies on open ground. The colonies are made up of family groups of parent birds and their young. The birds are packed tightly together for safety. As part of a crowd, eggs and chicks are less likely to be attacked by predators, such as foxes or herring gulls. A number of adult gulls may also join forces to drive enemies away from their offspring.

# FAMILY TO THE RESCUE

**Many animal parents go to great lengths to protect their offspring. They take their young along on food-finding expeditions and have various ways of conveying them to safety if they stray. Some parents even risk, or appear to risk, their own lives for their young.**

### Follow my leader
A female shrew may have up to six babies in one litter. As soon as the young are old enough, their mother takes them with her as she hunts for food. The first baby takes hold of the base of the mother's tail, and the others line up behind it. The young all keep in step as they run after her. They split up to feed, but if danger threatens, they immediately form their "caravan" again.

### Carried away
When faced with danger, the reaction of some animal parents is to pick up their young and carry them to safety. Many kinds of mammals, such as otters, dogs, and cats, behave in this way, picking up their offspring by the scruff of their necks. The baby's automatic response is to let its body go limp, so that it is easier to carry. It also goes quiet, so it does not give itself away by sounds.

Jacanas are tropical waterbirds. They get their nickname, "lily trotters," because their long toes allow them to walk across water lily leaves without sinking. The male jacana builds the nest, and raises and protects the chicks on his own. If danger threatens, some species of jacana carry their young to safety under their wings.

**Only the feet are visible as the male jacana carries his two chicks beneath his wing.**

**Mother rats carry their young too, but hold them by the loose skin on their backs.**

At some risk to herself, the female plover will feign injury to lead a predator such as a fox away from her eggs.

## What a mouthful

Some species of cichlid fish, called mouthbrooders, rear and protect their young inside their mouths. The eggs hatch inside the mother's mouth, and the young stay there until they are old enough to swim out and fend for themselves. Even then, at the first sign of danger, the mother opens her mouth wide and the young rush to safety inside. The mother keeps her mouth firmly closed until the threat has passed.

Young cichlids make short trips outside their mother's mouth, but do not stray far at first.

## Distraction display

Some birds who lay their eggs on the ground have a special way of luring predators away from their nest. It is called a distraction display. Female plovers lay their eggs on pebbly beaches. The eggs are well camouflaged, but if this does not fool a predator, the mother bird will try to distract its attention. She runs away from the nest, holding one wing as if it is broken. Thinking that this injured bird will be easy to catch, the predator follows. Suddenly, at a safe distance from the nest, she "recovers" and flies off.

# THE FAMILY MEAL

**Finding enough to eat plays a major part in an animal's family life. Some animals work in pairs or teams to gather food more efficiently. A great deal of family activity centers around providing and receiving food.**

## Baby food

Parent animals use up huge amounts of energy making sure that their young are well fed. Eurasian kingfishers may rear up to seven young in their nest tunnel in the riverbank. Each hatchling eats 15 or more fish a day. Between them, therefore, the parent birds may have to catch 100 fish a day, not counting the ones they need to feed themselves. Fish are presented to the nestlings head first, so that they are easier to swallow.

A female Ammophila wasp drags a caterpillar into the burrow, which may accommodate up to six eggs.

Ammophila wasps in the western deserts lay their eggs in underground burrows. The female paralyzes a caterpillar with its sting, and drags it into the burrow. Then it lays an egg in it. When the egg hatches, the grub has a ready meal of caterpillar meat to feed on. Because the caterpillar has been paralyzed, not killed, its meat is still fresh.

## Supplying drink

For desert animals, getting enough to drink is a major problem. Sand grouse have an ingenious way of providing their chicks with water. The male flies up to 50 miles to a water hole, where he soaks his breast feathers in water. These feathers are specially designed to hold water in the same way as a sponge. Then he flies back to the young birds. He encourages them to push under his body and suck the water off.

Mammals are the only animals that produce true milk to feed their young. But pigeons provide their nestlings with an unusual drink called "crop milk." This thick, white liquid is made in the adult's crop (part of the bird's gullet or throat). For the first few days of their lives, the nestlings live on this alone. They stick their heads inside their parent's mouth and suck the milk up. Both parents produce crop milk.

Adult pigeons' diet of seeds would be difficult for nestlings to digest. They are fed crop milk instead.

Kingfishers dive from perches above the water to catch fish. They are skilful divers and fishers. They need to be to keep their ravenous chicks well fed.

## Family hunting

Being part of a family can have great benefits when it comes to finding food. African hunting dogs work in teams to bring down their prey of antelope and wildebeest. An individual dog on its own would never be able to tackle such large prey. The team harass and snap at the animal's legs until it is too tired and weak to resist. The dogs have great stamina and will pursue their prey for several miles to wear it down. In terms of energy expended, it is more efficient for the whole pack to kill one large animal in a single hunt than for individual dogs to be constantly chasing after smaller animals that will provide only "snacks."

Hunting dogs snap at the heels of their prey until it is so tired that it can be pulled to the ground.

# FAMILY DISPUTES

**In any family, squabbles and disputes sometimes break out. Rivals compete to take charge of the group and for the attentions of a mate. Other families that trespass into a group's territory must be driven away. Play fighting is an important part of family life, too.**

### Defending territory

Many kinds of animals maintain and protect a particular area, called a territory, where they feed and breed. Animals defend their territories fiercely, driving out rival families or intruders. This is the cause of many disputes.

At breeding time, a male stickleback builds a nest for his mate's eggs. He defends it aggressively against intruders. If another male comes close, the nest owner will fan his fins and raise the spines on his back to make himself look threatening. If this doesn't work, the two fish may fight, biting each other until one slinks away.

Rival rat packs also use body language in disputes over territory. To warn away a rival group, the members of a pack fluff up their fur and stand sideways, making themselves appear bigger and more frightening than they actually are.

### Jostling for position

In many families, a hierarchy operates, in which some animals are senior and others junior. Senior members have more control and influence over the group, and often get priority in terms of sleeping places, food, and mates. Fights break out as more junior members try to work their way up the social order.

A male stickleback defends his nest territory, challenging trespassers who swim too close.

Male hippos are fiercely territorial. Adult males battle for control of the herd of females and young, and to defend their river territories. A fight between rivals may last for several hours. The males use their huge canine teeth as weapons, and can inflict fatal wounds on each other, despite their thick skins.

**Hippos wrestle and open their mouths to show off their teeth before a fight begins in earnest.**

Within a troop of baboons there may be several powerful males in charge. The baboon hierarchy is based on size and strength. Fights, or displays of threatening behavior, occur as the males jostle for position. The same animals cooperate with one another to defend their territory from rival troops.

**Puppies signal to each other before play-fighting that this is a game, not a real contest.**

## Fighting for fun

Mock fights are common among primates such as monkeys and apes, and among other mammals, such as many species of cats and dogs. Young lion and cheetah cubs, for example, go through the motions of fighting with their sisters and brothers. The cubs are quite capable of hurting each other with their sharp teeth and claws. But before the fight begins, they signal to each other that this is only play, not the real thing. Young animals seem to enjoy playing, but play also has a serious purpose. It helps to strengthen the bonds between the cubs and allows them to practice the hunting and fighting skills they will need later in life (see pages 8-9).

**An angry or aggressive baboon is an intimidating sight. Snarling and bared teeth are intended to scare rivals off. If this does not work, a fight may break out.**

# BREAKING AWAY

**Sooner or later, the time comes for young animals to fend for themselves. In many species this means the young must leave the family group to find a mate, establish their own territory, and start their own family.**

Young tawny owls practice their flying skills until they are confident enough to leave the nest.

The beaver kit holds on to its mother's tail as it practices its swimming.

## Leaving home

Young tawny owls are protected by their mother and fed by their father for several months after they hatch. Then they must leave the nest and their parents' woodland territory and find a territory of their own. The first independent months of a young owl's life are full of danger. About half of young tawny owls die in their first year, often of starvation, due to cold weather and lack of vacant territories. The size of territory these youngsters are able to establish depends on how much prey is available. Once established, the territory is fiercely defended, and the owner may live there for more than five years.

Beavers live in small, stable family groups, consisting of a pair of adults and their offspring. Young beavers, or kits, are not expected to leave the family until they are over two years old. During these first two years, the kits learn the skills essential for their survival – how to fish, and build their homes, called lodges, so that they can start a family of their own.

## Bachelor bulls

Elephant society is dominated by females, and the herd is led by the oldest female (see page 16). This type of society is called a matriarchy. Male elephants tend to live apart from the herd, and are only allowed to join it for mating. Young males stay with the herd from birth until they reach puberty, when they leave to live alone or in small, loose, "bachelor" groups. In contrast to the close bonds of the female herd, the ties between the males are weak, and there is little cooperation among members of a bachelor group.

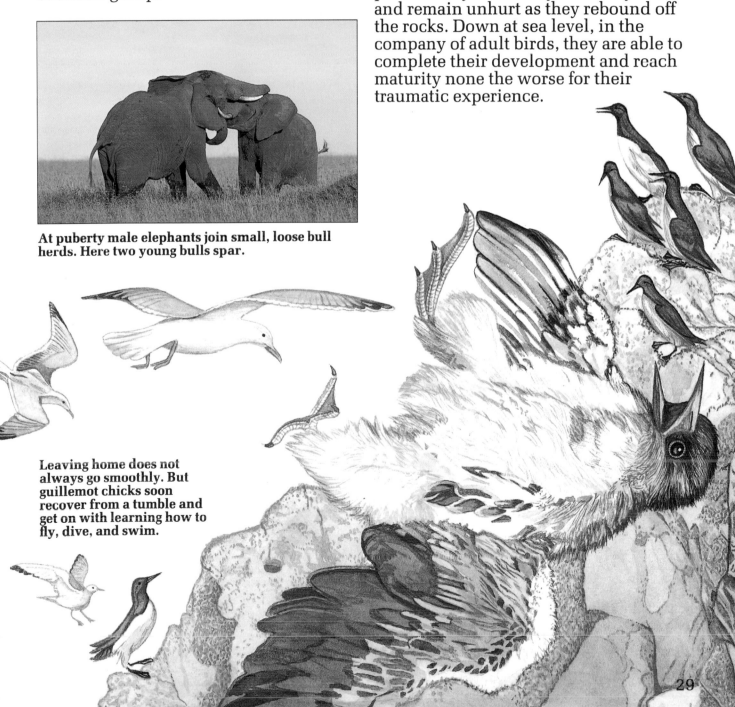

At puberty male elephants join small, loose bull herds. Here two young bulls spar.

Leaving home does not always go smoothly. But guillemot chicks soon recover from a tumble and get on with learning how to fly, dive, and swim.

## A bumpy ride

Guillemots breed in noisy, crowded colonies high on the narrowest of cliff ledges. When the chicks hatch, they are brought food by both parents and grow quickly. Many will be able to fly and leave the nest when they are about six weeks old. But some leave home prematurely. If half-grown chicks are attacked by gulls, they may throw themselves down the cliff face to escape. They cannot yet fly, and their tumbling fall seems sure to kill them. Surprisingly, however, they are protected by a thick layer of body fat, and remain unhurt as they rebound off the rocks. Down at sea level, in the company of adult birds, they are able to complete their development and reach maturity none the worse for their traumatic experience.

# SPOT IT YOURSELF

You can study animals and the way they behave almost anywhere. Learn to detect creatures by the signs they leave: burrow entrances, nests, footprints in mud or snow, hair caught in wire or branches, droppings, half-eaten leaves, and discarded shells. Approach animals downwind, so your scent does not give you away. When nature-spotting, keep as still and quiet as possible.

**Practical tips for nature-spotting**
Wear wind- and water-proof clothing in dull colors. Polaroid glasses reduce surface reflection for seeing underwater. A lens magnifies small animals and a camping mat gives some comfort.

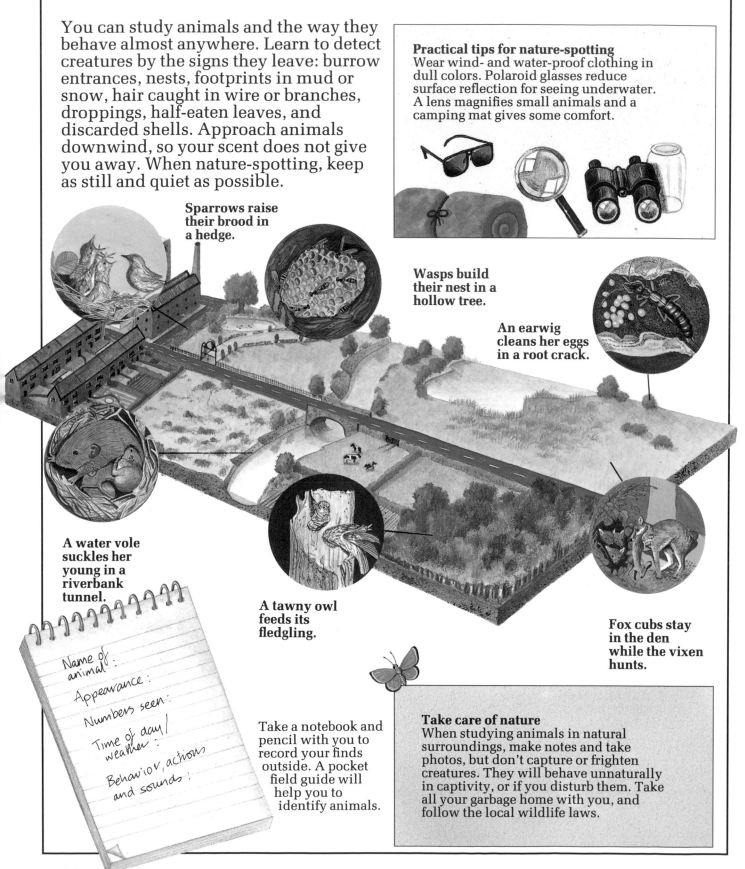

**Sparrows raise their brood in a hedge.**

**Wasps build their nest in a hollow tree.**

**An earwig cleans her eggs in a root crack.**

**A water vole suckles her young in a riverbank tunnel.**

**A tawny owl feeds its fledgling.**

**Fox cubs stay in the den while the vixen hunts.**

Name of animal:
Appearance:
Numbers seen:
Time of day/ weather:
Behavior, actions and sounds:

Take a notebook and pencil with you to record your finds outside. A pocket field guide will help you to identify animals.

**Take care of nature**
When studying animals in natural surroundings, make notes and take photos, but don't capture or frighten creatures. They will behave unnaturally in captivity, or if you disturb them. Take all your garbage home with you, and follow the local wildlife laws.

# GLOSSARY

**Altruism** The practice of animals helping each other at some cost to themselves.

**Behavior** The actions and movements of an animal, including sleeping, feeding, and courting.

**Colony** A group of animals of the same species that live and can breed together.

**Evolution** Change in species of living things over a period of time, usually many generations.

**Extended family** A family group which includes not only parents and their offspring, but aunts, uncles, cousins, and so on.

**Family** A group of animals either in a small, closely-knit unit or in a larger group, such as a flock.

**Genes** Coded instructions inside cells which pass on features and characteristics from parents to their offspring.

**Grooming** Keeping skin or fur clean and tidy and free from parasites.

**Harem** A breeding group in which one male mates with and dominates several females.

**Hierarchy** The graded organization of a family group in which some members are junior and others are senior.

**Imprinting** A kind of learning in young animals that helps them to recognize and follow their parent. Ducklings imprint on their mother and follow her wherever she goes.

**Incubation** The process by which birds, and other animals, hatch their eggs by sitting on them or otherwise protecting them.

**Instinctive** An action or behavior which is "in-built" from birth, and does not have to be learned.

**Kin selection** The process whereby closely-related animals help each other, to increase the chance of survival of common family genes.

**Mammal** An animal that has hair (fur) and feeds its young on milk.

**Matriarchy** An animal group which is led by an experienced female.

**Natural selection** The process whereby animals and plants which are best suited to the environment tend to be the ones that survive and breed. Over a long time, natural selection brings about evolution.

**Predator** An animal that lives by hunting others.

**Prey** An animal hunted for food by a predator.

**Primates** The group of animals which includes humans, apes, monkeys, lemurs and bushbabies.

**Species** A group of living things with the same characteristics, that can breed together.

**Territory** A patch of land or other area claimed by an animal, or group of animals, and defended against others, usually of its own kind. These defensive actions are known as territorial behavior.

# INDEX